Vegan Cooking:
50 Delectable Vegan Dessert Recipes

Gina 'The Veggie Goddess' Matthews

Copyright

TABLE OF CONTENTS

INTRODUCTION

I would like to thank my friends and family for being my test kitchen tasters. It really helps to have a diverse range of taste preferences sampling my kitchen creations, so that I may continue to grow and master flavor and texture profiles in the dishes I create.

Next, I'd like to include some vegan baking tips for those who may be new to the art of vegan cooking and baking, as well as to others who may not be aware of some tips and tricks that help make vegan cooking and baking more successful.

First and foremost, just like any other type of baking or cooking, always read a recipe all the way through before starting. This way, there won't be any surprises, and you'll know not just all the ingredients a recipe calls for, but also any potential ingredient swaps or substitutions you may choose or need to make.

Always take into consideration altitude and types of cooking appliances. Higher altitudes require baking and cooking time adjustments (typically longer), and certain ovens and stoves are more efficient than others, which means that you'll typically need to shorten the cooking or baking times. Know your appliances and altitudes, and be prepared to watch and adjust cooking and baking times accordingly.

Don't ever feel that however a recipe is laid out, that it is set in stone. Please always feel free to adjust a recipe, and make it your own. If you have a food allergy, by all means, either swap out a particular ingredient for a comparable one, or try just omitting it all-together from the recipe. Feel free to add or delete some of the called for spices, or swap out sweeteners, flours or recipe add-ins. Do remember though, that if you've made adjustments to a recipe and it doesn't turn out to your liking, it is most likely due to you either making too many substitutions, or one of your substitutions was an integral ingredient in the original recipe. If this happens, go back and try the recipe exactly as it calls for, and try to pinpoint where you might have made too many alterations.

When baking and cooking, I always recommend using raw sugar over sucanat. Many people think that raw sugar and sucanat are the same, but they are not. Sucanat (which stands for sugar cane natural) is a minimally processed cane sugar product and has a lesser effect on blood sugar than regular full-processed sugar. However, when it comes to cooking and baking with it, I have found that sucanat tends to absorb too much moisture from the liquid components in a recipe, and has the tendency to cause a dish to become too dry. Additionally, sucanat doesn't always dissolve readily. Raw sugar on the other hand, is very minimally processed, doesn't overly absorb moisture from a recipe, and does dissolve readily in liquids. However, if you just want to sprinkle a healthier sugar on your fruits or other dishes that don't require baking or cooking, then I would recommend sucanat over raw sugar, because the crystals are finer. I personally use 'Sugar in the Raw' brand raw sugar, but there are other quality brands available in your natural health food stores.

For recipes calling for pure maple syrup, do NOT substitute with pancake syrup. Real maple syrup comes in 'grade A', 'grade B' and 'grade C', and any of these grades of maple syrup will work just fine in these recipes. If you don't have, or can't find pure maple syrup, you can substitute with equal amounts of agave nectar.

When dessert recipes call for sea salt, do NOT omit it. Sea salt is not the same thing as commercially processed salt, which you should avoid like the plague. The purpose of sea salt in dessert recipes is to act as a flavor enhancer, helping to showcase and meld sweet flavor profiles from individual ingredients together. Additionally, adding sea salt to dessert recipes helps to 'cut' and balance out any acidic flavor tones, and when added to baked dessert recipes, sea salt also acts as a leveling agent.

When making any recipe that calls for tofu, always remember to drain, press and drain again before using. You always want to squeeze out the excess moisture in tofu before using, because it can be substantial enough to either alter the measured liquid components of a recipe, or the excess water will prevent the tofu from combining and melding with other called-for ingredients. You can either do this by hand, or purchase a tofu press. I simply place a block of tofu onto a cutting board after I remove it from the package, and using a spatula, gently press out any excess water. I then gently pat it dry with paper towels, and then the tofu is ready to use.

When recipes call for vegan margarine, I will sometimes specify to use vegan margarine in stick form instead of tub form. The reason is because tub margarine is whipped and has a high air content, whereas stick margarine is more dense, and in certain recipes you specifically need the density of the stick margarine. You can always use either, but it may affect the final outcome of your dessert.

And, lastly, have fun! Cooking and baking should always be fun, expressive and infused with lots of love.

Bon Veggie Appetit!

Gina 'The Veggie Goddess' Matthews

CHAPTER 1 – VEGAN CAKES AND CUPCAKES

3 Layered Sinful German Chocolate Cake

(preheat oven to 350 degrees and lightly grease and flour 3 round cake pans, then line each greased and floured cake pan with parchment paper)

Ingredients:

(cake)

6 ounces dried apricots

6 ounces water

3 tablespoons Ener-G egg replacer

¾ cup water

3 cups raw sugar

3 cups flour (all purpose)

1-1/4 cups cocoa powder

1 tablespoon baking soda

1-1/2 teaspoons aluminum-free baking powder

¾ teaspoon sea salt

1-1/2 cups oat milk

1 tablespoon white vinegar

2 teaspoons pure vanilla extract

(icing)

2 cups oat milk

2 cups raw sugar

1-1/2 teaspoons pure vanilla extract

5 tablespoons cornstarch

¼ cup water

2 cups coconut flakes

2 cups chopped nuts (walnuts or pecans)

In a bowl, soak the dried apricots in the 6 ounces of water until softened, and then transfer them to a blender and puree. In a large mixing bowl, whisk together the Ener-G egg replacer and ¾ cup water until frothy. Add in the apricot puree and sugar, and using an electric mixer, blend on medium-low speed until light in color and ingredients are well incorporated.

In a separate mixing bowl, sift together the flour, cocoa powder, baking soda, baking powder and salt. Slowly add dry flour mixture into the bowl with the moist ingredients, and blend on low until all ingredients are well blended, then set bowl aside. In a medium mixing bowl, stir together the 1-1/2 cups oat milk, vinegar and vanilla extract, and let stand for 10 minutes to 'cure'. After 10 minutes, pour the 'cured' milk mixture into the bowl with the batter, and stir well. Pour batter evenly into the three prepared cake pans, and bake for 25-30 minutes. (Toothpick should come out clean when inserted in the middle of the cake.) Remove from oven, and allow cakes to COOL COMPLETELY before removing from pans.

To make the icing, combine the oat milk, sugar and vanilla extract in a saucepan over medium heat, and cook while stirring until sugar is fully dissolved. In a small bowl, whisk together the cornstarch and ¼ cup water to form a paste, then slowly stir the cornstarch mixture into the saucepan with the other ingredients. Continue cooking and stirring over medium heat until mixture thickens. Remove from heat and stir in the coconut flakes and nuts. Continue stirring regularly, while the icing mixture cools. You want the icing mixture to cool before spreading onto cake. Spread a thin layer of the icing mixture on top of each layer of the cake, until you've assembled all 3 layers. Spread any excess icing across the top layer of the cake, or down the sides, using a spatula to press and gently adhere the icing to the sides of the cake.

Spiced Banana Raisin and Walnut Cake

(preheat oven to 375 degrees and lightly grease and flour bottom of 9x13 inch baking dish)

Ingredients:

2 cups flour (all-purpose)

2 teaspoons aluminum-free baking powder

1 teaspoon baking soda

1 tablespoon ground cinnamon

½ teaspoon ground nutmeg

¼ teaspoon ground cloves

½ teaspoon sea salt

1 cup non-dairy milk (any variety will work well with this recipe)

1 cup unsweetened applesauce

2 overripe bananas (peeled and diced – you want the peels to have brown freckling on them)

½ cup finely diced and pitted dates

1 tablespoon Ener-G egg replacer

6 tablespoons water

1 cup raisins

2 red or green apples (peeled and finely diced)

8

¾ cup finely chopped walnuts

In a mixing bowl, sift together the flour, baking powder, baking soda, cinnamon, nutmeg, clove and sea salt, until well blended. Next, in a blender, combine the non-dairy milk, applesauce, diced bananas, diced dates, Ener-G egg replacer and 6 tablespoons of water, and puree until smooth. Slowly pour the wet ingredients from the blender into the mixing bowl with the dry ingredients, and stir until all ingredients are moistened and well blended. Fold in the raisins and diced apples and pour batter into your prepared baking dish. Sprinkle the chopped nuts evenly across the top, and bake for 30-35 minutes, or until the cake start to pull away from the sides of the pan, and a toothpick comes out clean when inserted into the middle of the cake.

Coconut, Orange and Date Cake

(preheat oven to 350 degrees and lightly grease and flour bottom of 9x13 inch baking pan)

Ingredients:

1 cup flour (all-purpose)

2 cups whole wheat pastry flour

1 tablespoon aluminum-free baking powder

½ teaspoon sea salt

½-3/4 cup coconut flakes

2 cups coconut milk

1-1/2 cups pitted and rough chopped dates

½ cup coconut oil

1 large orange (first grate the zest from the orange, then cut in half and juice both halves)

In a large mixing bowl, sift together both the flours, baking powder and sea salt. Once combined, stir in the coconut flakes and set aside. Combine the coconut milk and chopped dates in a saucepan over medium heat, and simmer until dates become very soft. Remove from heat, allow mixture to cool slightly, and then combine the coconut milk-date mixture in a blender along with the coconut oil, grated orange zest and fresh squeezed orange juice. Puree until smooth, then slowly pour the coconut mixture into the bowl with dry ingredients and stir until all ingredients are moistened and well blended. The batter will be stiff, but if it's too stiff to work with, you can drizzle in just enough extra coconut milk or oil to help you work the batter. Just be careful not to add too much. Pour batter into your prepared baking dish, and bake for 35-45 minutes, or until cake is firm and the top is lightly golden brown. Allow cake to cool to room temperature before serving. Serve with an optional garnish of shredded or flaked coconut and/or a fresh orange wedge.

Bugs Bunny's Favorite Carrot Cake

(preheat oven to 350 degrees and lightly grease and flour a 9x13 inch baking dish)

Ingredients:

2-1/4 cups flour (all-purpose – but, you can also split 50/50 with whole wheat flour as well)

2 teaspoons baking soda

1 teaspoon aluminum-free baking powder

2-1/4 teaspoons ground cinnamon

1 teaspoon pumpkin pie spice

1 teaspoon sea salt

¾ cup packed brown sugar

¾ cup raw sugar

6 tablespoons water

4-1/2 teaspoons Ener-G egg replacer

1 teaspoon pure vanilla extract

1 cup canola oil

2 cups finely grated carrots

1 can (14 ounce) crushed pineapple (drained)

1 cup coconut flakes

1 cup raisins

½-3/4 cup crushed walnuts (optional)

(frosting)

1 package (8 ounce) vegan plain cream cheese (softened to room temperature)

1/3 cup vegan margarine (softened to room temperature)

2 cups powdered sugar

1 teaspoon pure vanilla extract

In a large mixing bowl, sift together the flour, baking soda, baking powder, cinnamon, pumpkin pie spice and salt, and then set aside. In a separate mixing bowl, using an electric mixer on low speed beat together the 6 tablespoons of water with the 4-1/2 teaspoons of Ener-G egg replacer until mixture becomes light and creamy. Continue beating at low speed, while adding in both of the sugars, vanilla extract and canola oil. Slowly add in the dry ingredients into the moist ingredients, and beat just until all ingredients are moistened and well blended. By hand, stir in the carrots, pineapple, coconut flakes, raisins and walnuts until evenly distributed, then pour batter into your prepared baking dish. Bake for 40-45 minutes, or until a toothpick comes out clean when inserted in the center of the cake. Remove from oven and allow cake to cool completely before frosting.

To make the frosting, I highly recommend mixing the ingredients by hand instead of using an electric mixer. I find that using an electric mixer tends to thin out the frosting too much, but if you take an extra couple minutes to mix the frosting by hand, the texture comes out just perfect. Once the cake has fully cooled, and you've mixed together the 4 frosting ingredients, go ahead and spread the frosting across the top of your carrot cake. (Note: If you prefer a thicker carrot cake, you can bake this in a 9x9 square pan, and adjust the baking time by a few extra minutes. Just remember to check the cake's doneness with a toothpick check.)

Pineapple Right-Side-Up Cake

(preheat oven to 350 degrees and generously grease the bottom of a 8x8 inch baking dish)

Ingredients:

1 can (20 ounce) unsweetened pineapple rings (drain and reserve the juice)

½ cup packed brown sugar

1-1/2 cups flour (all-purpose)

1 cup raw sugar

1 teaspoon baking soda

½ teaspoon sea salt

1/3 cup canola oil

1 tablespoon vinegar (white)

Arrange the pineapple rings on the bottom of your well greased baking dish, and then sprinkle the brown sugar evenly over the top. Pour the reserved pineapple juice into a liquid measuring cup (should be about ½-3/4 cup worth), and add enough water to equal 1 cup liquid. Pour the pineapple liquid into a mixing bowl, whisk in the canola oil and vinegar, and set bowl aside. In a separate mixing bowl, sift together the flour, sugar, baking soda and salt. Once combined, stir continuously while slowly adding in the wet ingredients and mix until all ingredients are moistened and well combined. Pour batter evenly across arranged pineapple slices, and bake for 55-60 minutes, until top is golden brown, and toothpick comes out clean when inserted in the middle of the cake. Remove from oven, and allow cake to cool completely before removing from pan. Once cake is fully cooled, use a butter knife to carefully separate the cake edges from the pan, place a flat serving board on top of the cake pan, and quickly flip the pan over so the cake releases from the pan and sets onto the serving board.

Why is it called Pineapple-Right-Side-Up-Cake? Because when you flip it over after baking, the pineapple rings are right side up. (Tip: Be sure to grease your baking dish generously (use vegan margarine) before arranging the cake layers, otherwise, your cake may stick to the pan.)

Chocolate Cinnamon Cake with Espresso Glaze

(preheat oven to 350 degrees and lightly grease and flour a 9x13 inch baking dish)

Ingredients:

8 ounces silken tofu (firm)

2 cups raw sugar

¾ cup canola oil

1 cup water

1 tablespoon pure vanilla extract

2 cups flour (all-purpose)

¾ cup unsweetened cocoa powder

2 teaspoons ground cinnamon

1 teaspoon baking soda

1 teaspoon cream-of-tartar

Pinch of sea salt

(glaze)

¼ cup canola oil (may substitute with same amount of vegan margarine)

¼ cup unsweetened cocoa powder

3 tablespoons water

1 teaspoon instant espresso powder

1-1/2 cups raw sugar

1 teaspoon pure vanilla extract

Ground cinnamon to sprinkle on top

In a large mixing bowl, using an electric mixer on medium speed, blend the tofu and 2 cups of raw sugar until mixture starts to become tacky. Increase mixer speed to high, and continue beating until mixture starts to become shiny and has the consistency of thick syrup. Add in the oil, water and vanilla extract and beat until all ingredients are well combined, then set bowl aside. In a separate mixing bowl, sift together the flour, cocoa powder, cinnamon, baking soda, cream of tartar and sea salt. Once combined, slowly fold the dry ingredients into the bowl with the wet mixture and blend until all ingredients are moistened. Pour batter into your prepared baking dish, and bake until toothpick comes out clean when inserted in the middle, about 40-50 minutes. Remove from oven and place on wire rack to fully cool.

To make the glaze, combine all the glaze ingredients (EXCEPT for the vanilla) in a saucepan over medium heat, and whisk continuously as mixture cooks and becomes shiny and smooth. Remove from heat, stir in the vanilla and let cool for 10 minutes or more before using. Once cake has completely cooled, give the glaze a thorough stir to blend, and then spread evenly across the top. Finish with a sprinkling of ground cinnamon on top of the glaze layer, cut and serve.

Coconut Vanilla Cupcakes with Coconut Frosting

(preheat oven to 350 degrees and grease or line 2 muffin tin pans)

Ingredients:

1-1/2 cups coconut milk (unsweetened)

1 tablespoon vinegar (white)

1/3 cup canola oil (or coconut oil)

¼ cup pure maple syrup (do NOT use pancake syrup)

2 teaspoons pure vanilla extract

2-1/4 cups flour (all-purpose)

½ teaspoon baking soda

1 cup raw sugar

½ teaspoon sea salt

½ cup coconut flakes

(frosting)

1 cup vegan margarine OR vegan shortening (softened to room temperature)

¼ cup coconut milk

1 teaspoon coconut extract (may substitute with vanilla extract)

3 – 3-1/2 cups powdered sugar

In a large mixing bowl, whisk together the coconut milk, vinegar, oil, maple syrup and vanilla extract, and then set bowl aside. In a separate mixing bowl, sift together the flour, baking soda, sugar and sea salt. Once combined, using an electric hand mixer beat on medium while slowly adding in the wet ingredients, until well blended and batter is fluffy and smooth, about 2 minutes. Fill each cupcake cup 2/3'rds full with batter, and bake for 13-16 minutes, or until toothpick comes out clean when inserted in middle. Remove from oven and let cupcakes stand for 5 minutes, before removing from tin, and then transfer them to a wire rack to cool completely. Make sure cupcakes are fully cooled before frosting.

To make frosting, using an electric mixer, beat the vegan margarine (vegan shortening) at medium speed for 2-3 minutes. Add the coconut milk and extract, and beat for an additional 5 minutes. You need the long beating time, as this makes the frosting nice and fluffy. Lastly, slowly add in the powdered sugar (start with 3 cups and add more as needed) and keep mixing until you get desired consistency. Chill frosting in the fridge for 30-45 minutes before using. Once cupcakes are fully cooled, frost and serve.

Chocolate Puffed Rice Cupcakes with Chocolate Frosting

(line a 10-12 count muffin tin with FOIL paper liners)

Ingredients:

¼-1/2 cup vegan margarine

4-3/4 cups vegan marshmallows

½ teaspoon pure vanilla extract

5-1/2 cups puffed rice cereal

1 cup vegan chocolate chips (semi-sweet)

(frosting)

¼ cup cocoa powder (unsweetened)

½ cup vegan margarine (softened to room temperature)

2 cups powdered sugar

2 tablespoons non-dairy milk (soy, rice or coconut work best for this recipe)

2 teaspoons pure vanilla extract

Pinch of sea salt

Melt the margarine in a large saucepan over medium-low heat. Add in the marshmallows and stir continuously until marshmallows are melted and fully blended with the margarine. Remove from heat and stir in the vanilla extract. Immediately fold in the puffed rice cereal and vegan chocolate chips, and blend until all ingredients are evenly coated. Fill each foil lined cup all the way full with the cupcake mixture (you want each cupcake to be slightly domed) and let them cool for at least 2-3 hours before frosting and serving.

To make frosting, combine all frosting ingredients in a blender, and puree until smooth and well blended. Chill frosting in the fridge for 30-45 minutes, before frosting your cooled cupcakes. (Note: You want to keep these cupcakes in a tightly sealed container, and eat within 2 days, as they tend to dry out by day 3.)

Mango and Macadamia Nut Cupcakes with Rum Frosting

(preheat oven to 350 degrees and grease or paper line 2 cupcake tins)

Ingredients:

1-3/4 cups flour (all-purpose)

1 teaspoon baking soda

1 cup raw sugar

½ cup coconut oil

1 tablespoon vinegar (white)

1 teaspoon pure vanilla extract

¼ teaspoon coconut extract

1 cup (8 ounces) fresh mango (pureed in blender, and measured after pureed)

¾ cup coconut flakes (unsweetened)

¾-1 cup macadamia nuts (finely chopped in blender or grinder, and measured after chopped)

(frosting)

½ cup vegan margarine (softened to room temperature)

1 firm, slightly green banana (peeled and mashed)

½ teaspoon freshly squeezed lemon juice

1 teaspoon pure vanilla extract

1 teaspoon dark rum

4-6 cups powdered sugar (sifted first)

In a large mixing bowl, sift together the flour, baking soda and sugar, and then set bowl aside. In a separate mixing bowl, whisk together the coconut oil, vinegar, vanilla extract, coconut extract and mango puree. Once combined, slowly add in the dry mixture and blend just until all ingredients are moistened and well incorporated. Fold in the coconut flakes and chopped macadamia nuts, and then fill each cupcake cup 2/3'rds full with batter. Bake for 25-30 minutes, or until toothpick comes out clean when inserted in the middle. Remove from oven and allow cupcakes to cool completely on a wire rack.

To make frosting, in a large mixing bowl cream together the vegan margarine, mashed banana, lemon juice, vanilla extract and rum. Continue beating, while slowly adding in the powdered sugar, until desired consistency is reached. Start with 4 cups, then add more as needed. Chill frosting in the fridge while cupcakes are cooling, to further solidify the consistency. Once cupcakes are fully cooled, frost and serve.

Coffee Cake Cupcakes

(preheat oven to 350 degrees and grease or line 2 cupcake tins)

Ingredients:

2 cups flour (all-purpose and un-sifted to help give the cupcakes a coffee cake texture)

¾ cup rolled oats (do NOT use instant)

1/3 cup packed brown sugar

1 tablespoon aluminum-free baking powder

2 teaspoons ground cinnamon

½ teaspoon ground nutmeg

¼ teaspoon ground ginger

Pinch of sea salt

½ cup vegan margarine (softened to room temperature)

1 cup natural apple juice (no sugar added)

In a large mixing bowl, stir together the un-sifted flour, ½ of the rolled oats, brown sugar, baking powder, cinnamon, nutmeg, ginger and salt. Scoop out ½ cup of the blended mixture into a separate mixing bowl, and to the ½ cup of blended mixture add in the remaining rolled oats. Using a fork, cut in 2 tablespoons of the margarine to the rolled oats mixture, until it forms a 'crumble-like' consistency, and then set aside.

Cut the remaining margarine into the mixing bowl with the flour mixture, and then stir in the apple juice until all ingredients are moistened and well combined. Fill each cupcake cup 2/3'rds full with batter (you'll have enough for 1-1/2 to 2 cupcake tins), then evenly divide and top each cupcake with the reserved oat mixture. Bake for 20-30 minutes, or until toothpick comes out clean when inserted in the middle. Remove from oven, and allow cupcakes to cool to room temperature on a wire rack before serving.

CHAPTER 2 – VEGAN COOKIES

Spiced Nuts and Berries Oatmeal Cookies

(preheat oven to 400 degrees and line a large cookie sheet with parchment paper)

Ingredients:

6 tablespoons water

2-1/2 tablespoons ground flaxseed

2 cups flour (all-purpose)

1 teaspoon baking soda

½ teaspoon aluminum-free baking powder

½ teaspoon sea salt

2 pinches of ground cinnamon

1 pinch of ground nutmeg

1 cup vegan margarine (softened to room temperature)

2 teaspoons real vanilla extract (may substitute with almond extract)

1 cup raw sugar

1 cup packed brown sugar

2 cups uncooked rolled oats (do not use instant)

1 cup dried cranberries (give them a quick rough chop)

1 cup crushed pecans (may substitute with crushed walnuts)

In a small bowl, whisk together the ground flaxseed and water, and let it sit to 'gel up' while you are preparing the rest of the ingredients.

In a mixing bowl, whisk together the flour, baking soda, baking powder, sea salt, cinnamon and nutmeg, and set aside. In a separate large mixing bowl, using an electric mixer, beat together the softened margarine (make sure it is softened, but not liquefied) and gelled-up flaxseed mixture. Once blended, add in the vanilla extract and sugar, and beat for an additional 1 minute. Gradually add in the dry flour mixture, while beating on low speed, until all ingredients are well blended. (cookie dough will be thick)

By hand, stir in the rolled oats, dried cranberries and crushed pecans. Shape dough into tablespoon sized balls and line 2 inches apart on parchment-lined cookie sheet. Bake until golden browned (about 8-10 minutes), remove from oven and let cool for 2-3 minutes before removing from cookie sheet.

Addictive Chocolate Chip Cookies

(preheat oven to 360 degrees and lightly grease a large cookie sheet)

Ingredients:

2-1/4 cups flour (all-purpose)

1 teaspoon baking soda

1 teaspoon sea salt

¾ cup raw sugar

¾ cup of packed brown sugar

1 cup vegan margarine (softened to room temperature)

1 teaspoon pure vanilla extract

1/3 cup natural applesauce (no sugar added)

1 bag (12 ounces) vegan semi-sweet chocolate chips (may substitute vegan carob chips)

In a large mixing bowl, beat together both the sugars, vegan margarine, vanilla extract and applesauce until smooth and creamy. In a separate mixing bowl, whisk together the flour, baking soda and sea salt, then slowly fold into the mixing bowl with the moist ingredients, and blend until all ingredients are well incorporated and batter is smooth. By hand, stir in the chocolate chips, and then drop dough by rounded teaspoonfuls 1 inch apart, onto prepared cookie sheet. Bake until lightly

222

browned (about 10-15 minutes) and allow cookies to cool for 2-3 minutes before removing from cookie sheet.

(Tips: If the batter is too stiff, had in another ¼ cup applesauce. Baking at 375 degrees tends to burn the bottoms of the cookies, which is why I adjusted the baking temperature to 360 degrees, but of course, all ovens will vary.)

Magnificent Molasses Cookies

(preheat oven to 325 degrees and use a quality non-stick baking sheet)

Ingredients:

1 cup packed brown sugar

¾ cup canola oil (may substitute ½ cup natural applesauce + ¼ cup canola oil)

¼ cup unsulfured molasses

3 tablespoons 'Ener-G' egg replacer

2-1/4 cups flour (all-purpose)

2 teaspoons baking soda

1 teaspoon ground cinnamon

1 teaspoon ground ginger

½ teaspoon ground cloves

¼ teaspoon sea salt

3-4 tablespoons raw sugar (for coating)

In a large mixing bowl, using an electric mixer, blend together the sugar, oil, molasses and Ener-G egg replacer until smooth and creamy. In a separate mixing bowl, whisk together the flour baking soda, ground cinnamon, ginger, cloves and sea salt, until well blended, then slowly add in the dry mixture into the moist mixture, and continue blending on low speed until all ingredients are well incorporate. Roll the dough into tablespoon sized balls and give a quick roll in the raw sugar to coat. Line the prepared dough balls 1 inch apart on cookie sheet, and bake for 12-14 minutes. Cookies will look slightly dry when done. If you prefer crunchy molasses cookies instead of chewy ones, increase baking time by 1-2 minutes. Allow cookies to cool 2-3 minutes before removing from cookie sheet.

Heavenly Lemon Cookies

(preheat oven to 350 degrees and lightly grease a large cookie sheet)

Ingredients:

1 tablespoon ground flaxseed

3 tablespoons water

½ cup non-dairy milk (rice or coconut milk taste best

with this recipe)

2 teaspoons fresh-squeezed lemon juice

1-3/4 cups flour (all-purpose)

1 teaspoon aluminum-free baking powder

¼ teaspoon baking soda

¼ teaspoon sea salt

½ cup vegan margarine (softened to room temperature)

¾ cup raw sugar

1 teaspoon fresh-grated lemon rind

Glaze Topping (optional)

¾ cup raw sugar

¼ cup fresh squeezed lemon juice

In a small bowl, stir together the ground flaxseeds and water, and set aside to allow mixture to thicken. In another small bowl, you'll be making a vegan 'buttermilk', by stirring together the non-dairy milk and 2 teaspoons lemon juice, and then set aside.

In a medium mixing bowl, whisk together the flour, baking powder, baking soda and sea salt. In a separate large mixing bowl, beat the vegan margarine for about 30-40 seconds on medium speed, then add in the sugar and beat until fluffy. Continue mixing, and slowly add in the flaxseed mixture, the 'buttermilk' mixture, lemon rind and dry flour mixture, and beat until all ingredients are well incorporated and batter is smooth.

Drop dough by rounded teaspoonfuls 1 inch apart onto prepared cookie sheet, and bake for 12-14 minutes. Remove cookies immediately from baking sheet and transfer onto a wire rack for cooling. <u>For the optional cookie glaze</u>: stir together the ¾ cup sugar and ¼ cup lemon juice while cookies are baking, and using a basting or pastry brush, lightly 'glaze' each cookie top while cookie is still warm and cooling on the wire rack.

Sugar Cookies with 'Magic Fairy Dust'

(preheat oven to 350 degrees and line a large cookie sheet with parchment paper)

<u>Ingredients:</u>

2 tablespoons ground flaxseed

1/3 cup water

3-3/4 cups flour (all-purpose)

1-1/2 teaspoons aluminum-free baking powder

¾ teaspoon sea salt

1 cup vegan margarine (softened to room temperature)

2 cups powdered sugar (also called confectioners sugar)

3 tablespoons non-dairy milk (works best with either coconut or rice milk)

2 teaspoons pure vanilla extract

½ teaspoon almond extract

'Magic Fairy Dust'

Equal parts of raw sugar, ground cardamom and ground cinnamon (for dusting cookies while they are cooling)

In a small bowl, whisk together the ground flaxseed and water, and set aside to allow mixture to thicken up. In a medium bowl, whisk together the flour, baking powder and sea salt and set aside. In a large mixing bowl, using an electric mixer beat together the margarine, sugar, non-dairy milk and both the extracts for 1 minute on low-medium speed. Slowly add in the dry flour mixture a little at a time, while still blending, followed by the thickened flaxseed mixture, and beat until all ingredients are well incorporated and batter is smooth and creamy. Dough needs to chill in the fridge for 1-2 hours before baking. If you will be using cookie cutters, you can just shape dough into one large ball and cover tightly with plastic wrap. If you will be making cut round cookies, divide the dough into two equal halves, and shape into cylinder tubes before wrapping with plastic and placing in the fridge.

After 1-2 hours, remove your chilled dough and either roll out with a rolling pin and cut with cookie cutters ¼ inch thick, or slice your dough tubes into ¼ inch rounds, and place 1 inch apart on parchment lined cookie sheets. Bake until lightly browned (about 16-20 minutes), then remove from oven and immediately transfer onto wire racks to cool.

While cookies are baking, whisk together your 'magic fairy dust' of equal parts sugar, cardamom and cinnamon, and immediately dust your just baked cookies with the 'fairy mixture', which will then 'set' onto the cookies as they cool.

Crazy for Coconut Macaroons

(preheat oven to 350 degrees and line a large cookie sheet with parchment paper)

Ingredients:

1 cup coconut milk (do NOT use 'lite' coconut milk-you need the full fat version)

¼ cup raw sugar

¼ teaspoon sea salt

2 tablespoons flour (all-purpose)

1 teaspoon pure vanilla extract

2 cups sweetened shredded coconut (do NOT use flaked coconut)

(If you can't find sweetened shredded coconut that does not contain corn syrup, you may substitute with 2 cups unsweetened shredded coconut and an additional 1/3 cup raw sugar.)

Optional: melted vegan chocolate chips for drizzled

topping

In a saucepan over medium heat, combine the coconut milk, ¼ cup raw sugar and sea salt and bring to a low boil. Once mixture comes to a soft boil, immediately whisk in the flour, and stir continuously while keeping at a low boil for 2 minutes. Reduce heat to medium-low, and continue cooking until mixture becomes just slightly thinner than a pudding (about 4-6 minutes). Remove from heat, and stir in the vanilla extract and shredded coconut (shredded coconut & sugar if using unsweetened coconut), until well blended.

Drop by rounded teaspoonfuls onto parchment lined cookie sheet, and bake until tops are golden brown (about 13-16 minutes). Remove from oven and wait 2-3 minutes before transferring cookies to a wire rack to finish cooling. Once cookies are transferred onto wire rack, you may drizzle them with melted vegan chocolate chips (optional).

Banana Nut Cookies

(preheat oven to 350 degrees and lightly grease a large cookie sheet)

Ingredients:

1-1/4 cups flour (all-purpose)

½ teaspoon baking soda

1 teaspoon aluminum-free baking powder

½ teaspoon sea salt

½ cup raw sugar

Just under ½ cup canola oil (you want to use between 1/3-1/2 cup)

½ teaspoon pure vanilla extract

4 tablespoons non-dairy milk (oat or nut milk work best for this recipe)

1 large, very ripe banana (mashed)

1 large handful of crushed walnuts (you may substitute with mini vegan chocolate chips)

* You can also add a pinch of ground cinnamon to this recipe, for an extra flavor boost.

In a medium mixing bowl, whisk together the flour, baking soda, baking powder and sea salt and set aside. In a large mixing bowl, using an electric hand mixer on low speed, beat together the sugar, oil, vanilla extract and non-dairy milk. Slowly add in the mashed banana and dry flour mixture, and beat until all ingredients are well incorporated. By hand, stir in the crushed nuts (or mini chocolate chips), and drop batter by rounded teaspoonfuls onto prepared cookie sheet. Bake until tops are golden brown (about 9-12 minutes), and let cookie sit for 2-3 minutes before removing from cookie sheet.

Old Fashioned Oatmeal Raisin Cookies

(preheat oven to 360 degrees and lightly grease a large cookie sheet)

Ingredients:

¼ cup of packed brown sugar

¼ cup raw sugar

¾ cup natural applesauce (unsweetened)

¼ teaspoon pure vanilla extract

1 cup flour (all-purpose)

1 teaspoon aluminum-free baking powder

½ teaspoon sea salt

½ teaspoon ground cinnamon

1 cup rolled oats (do not use instant oats)

½ cup raisins (rough chopped)

*Optional add-ins: 1/3 cup finely crushed walnuts / ½ teaspoon freshly grated orange peel

In mixing bowl, whisk together the flour, baking powder, sea salt and cinnamon, and set aside. In a separate large mixing bowl, stir together the sugars, applesauce and vanilla extract until well combined.

Slowly fold in the dry flour mixture, mixing until all ingredients are moistened and well incorporated. Drop batter by rounded spoonfuls onto prepared cookie sheet, and bake until tops are golden brown (about 12-16 minutes). Allow cookies to sit for 2-3 minutes before removing from cookie sheet.

*Note: These cookies will come out with a slight muffin consistency. Baking at 375 degrees tends to bake the cookies unevenly (done on the outside, but not in the middle), which is why I lowered the oven temperature for this recipe to 360 degrees.

CHAPTER 3 – VEGAN PUDDINGS AND PIES

Luscious Lemon Pie

Ingredients:

1 prebaked pie crust

2 cups water

1 cup raw sugar

¾ cup silken tofu (firm)

6 tablespoons cornstarch

1 tablespoon canola oil

¼ teaspoon sea salt

½ cup fresh squeezed lemon juice (2-4 lemons depending on size)

2 teaspoons finely grated lemon peel

Combine water, sugar, tofu, cornstarch, oil and salt in a blender, and blend until smooth. Transfer mixture into a saucepan, and bring to a low boil over medium heat, while whisking continuously. Continue cooking at a low boil until mixture begins to thicken, then reduce heat to low and cook for an additional 1 minute. Remove from heat and stir in the lemon juice and grated lemon peel. Allow mixture to cool a bit before transferring into pie shell, cover with waxed paper (to prevent skin from forming) and refrigerate for at least 8 hours, or overnight.

Whipped Topping:

(make this just before you are ready to serve your pie)

¾ cup silken tofu (soft)

2 tablespoons pure maple syrup (do NOT use pancake syrup)

2 teaspoons oil (use either canola or walnut)

1 teaspoon pure vanilla extract

Pinch of ground nutmeg

Combine all whipped topping ingredients together in a blender, and blend on high speed until mixture is smooth and creamy. Remove waxed paper from pie, gently spread with whipped topping and serve.

Easy Chocolate Peanut Butter Cup Pie

Ingredients:

1 prepared graham cracker crust (regular or chocolate)

1 package (12.3 ounce) of silken tofu (firm or extra-firm)

1 cup melted vegan chocolate chips (*Measure 1 cup of chocolate AFTER it is melted)

1-2 ripe bananas (do not use bananas if they still have green spots on peel)

¾ cup natural peanut butter (creamy variety)

1-2 tablespoons pure maple syrup (to taste for sweetness)

Cut the bananas into ¼ inch rounds, and use them to line the bottom of the graham cracker crust. Overlap as needed, to make sure crust bottom is fully covered.

After first making sure, that the tofu is well drained and patted dry with paper towels, rough chop the tofu, and combine with the remaining ingredients in a blender or food processor. Puree until mixture is smooth and creamy, and then pour into your prepared crust. Make a loose tent cover using aluminum foil, and chill in the fridge for at least 3 hours, to allow pie to 'set'.

Almond Lemon Cheesecake (I put this recipe in the pie section, because it's not really a cake)

(preheat oven to 350 degrees)

Ingredients:

(crust)

2 cups graham cracker crumbs

¼ cup pure maple syrup (do NOT use pancake syrup)

¼ teaspoon almond extract

(filling)

1 pound firm or extra-firm silken tofu (each package is 12.3 ounces, so use 1 & 1/3 packages)

1/3 cup raw sugar

1 tablespoon almond butter

½ teaspoon sea salt

1-2 tablespoons fresh squeezed lemon juice (to desired lemon taste preference)

½ teaspoon fresh grated lemon peel (fresh grated peel is key over dehydrated lemon peel)

½ teaspoon almond extract

2 tablespoons cornstarch (dissolve in the rice/coconut milk)

2 tablespoons rice or coconut milk

In a small mixing bowl, combine the graham crackers, maple syrup and almond extract, until mixture becomes tacky and slightly crumbly. Press the mixture evenly into a 9 'inch pie pan to form the crust, and bake in preheated oven for 5 minutes. Remove and let cool while preparing filling.

Combine all the filling ingredients in a blender or food processor, and puree until smooth and creamy, about 30-60 seconds. Pour mixture into the cooked crust, return to oven, and bake until top becomes lightly browned, about 30-35 minutes. Remove from oven and allow pie to cool to room temperature, cover with waxed paper and chill in the fridge for a minimum of 3 hours before serving. This will allow the pie to fully set.

Orange Zested Berry Pie

(preheat oven to 350 degrees)

Ingredients:

1 9 inch prepared pie crust (found in dairy section of grocery store)

1 bag (typically 13 ounce) of cranberries (found in produce section)

1 bag (12 or 13 ounce) frozen blueberries

1 large orange

½ cup raw sugar

½ teaspoon pure vanilla extract

1 teaspoon cornstarch

Gently roll out and line a 9 inch pie plate with the prepared pie crust. Using a grater, first zest the orange, then cut orange in half and squeeze out the juice from both halves. Put both the orange zest and freshly squeezed juice into a large mixing bowl, stir in all the remaining ingredients, and toss well to evenly coat all ingredients with the sugar. Pour berry mixture into the crust-lined pie pan, and bake for 25-30 minutes. Remove from oven and allow pie to cool at room temperature before serving. (This is a great vegan pie recipe to serve during the holiday season.)

Death by Decadent Chocolate Pudding

Ingredients:

1-3/4 cups raw sugar

1 cup unsweetened baking cocoa

½ cup flour (all purpose)

5 cups non-dairy milk (any will work, but I prefer almond or oat milk for this recipe)

1-1/2 tablespoons pure vanilla extract

2 pinches of sea salt

In a large saucepan, whisk together the sugar, baking cocoa and flour BEFORE turning on the heat, to incorporate the dry ingredients. Next whisk in the milk and stir to moistening all the ingredients. Turn on the heat to medium, and whisk continuously while bringing mixture up to a low boil. Once mixture comes to a boil, reduce heat slightly and continue whisking as pudding starts to thicken, about 1-2 minutes. Remove pan from heat, stir in the vanilla extract and sea salt, and let pudding cool slightly before transferring into individual serving cups. Cover serving cups with plastic wrap and chill in the fridge for at least 2 hours before serving. May be served with an optional garnish of fresh fruit, shredded coconut, chopped nuts or vegan whipped topping.

Gingerbread Cookie Pudding

Ingredients:

2/3 cup raw sugar

6 tablespoons cornstarch

Couple pinches of sea salt

1 tablespoon + 1 teaspoon ground cinnamon (equals 4 teaspoons)

2 teaspoons ground ginger

¼ teaspoon ground nutmeg

4 cups non-dairy milk (I prefer rice or coconut milk for this recipe)

3-4 tablespoons unsulfured molasses

In a large saucepan, whisk together the sugar, cornstarch, salt and spices BEFORE turning on the heat, to incorporate all the dry ingredients. Add in ½ cup of the non-dairy milk, and stir until mixture forms a thick goo-like consistency. Turn the heat on the medium, add in the remaining non-dairy milk, and whisk continuously, until pudding thickens, about 5-8 minutes. About midway through the cooking, drizzle in the molasses (use 3 tablespoons for a spiced pudding flavor, and 4 tablespoons for a distinctive gingerbread cookie flavor). It is important that you stir the mixture continuously while cooking. Remove pan from heat and allow the pudding to cool a bit, before transferring into individual pudding cups. Cover the cups with plastic wrap, and chill in the fridge for a minimum of 3 hours. Serve with an optional garnish of drizzled non-dairy milk and gingerbread cookies.

Easy Banana Nut Pudding

<u>Ingredients:</u>

20 ounces silken tofu (soft)

12 ounces silken tofu (firm)

2 large, very ripe bananas (do not use if there are any green patches on the peel)

1 cup raw sugar

½ cup non-dairy milk (any variety will work for this recipe)

4 teaspoons pure vanilla extract

½ cup finely crushed walnuts (optional)

Make sure all your tofu is well drained and patted dry before using. Combine all ingredients, EXCEPT for the nuts, in a blender or food processor, and puree until mixture is smooth and creamy. Toss in the crushed nuts, and blend for just a few seconds. Just long enough to evenly distribute the nuts in the pudding mixture. Transfer pudding into individual serving cups, cover with plastic wrap, and chill in the fridge for a minimum of 3 hours before serving.

Cinnamon Coconut Rice Pudding

<u>Ingredients:</u>

2 cans (16 ounces each) coconut milk

Raw sugar to taste for sweetness (I typically use about 1/3-1/2 cup raw sugar)

1 cup unsweetened shredded coconut (finely chopped)

4 cups cooked white rice (I typically use basmati or jasmine rice, but any will work)

2-1/2 teaspoons pure vanilla extract

Couple large pinches of ground cinnamon

3/4 cup raisins (optional)

In a large saucepan, heat the coconut milk over medium heat until it comes to a simmer. Add in the sugar, and stir until sugar is fully dissolved. Add in the shredded coconut and cooked white rice, and continue cooking until mixture starts to thicken. Be careful not to overcook, otherwise the pudding will get too dry. The rice will continue to absorb the coconut milk as it cools. Remove from heat and stir in the vanilla extract, cinnamon and raisins. Allow pudding to cool slightly, before transferring into individual serving cups. Cover with plastic wrap and chill in the fridge until ready to serve. This pudding is also good eaten warm for breakfast, instead of oatmeal. If your pudding ever turns out too dry, just serve with a drizzle of coconut milk, or other non-dairy milk, to moisten. And, you can also serve this pudding with an optional garnish of extra raisins and/or crushed nuts.

CHAPTER 4 – VEGAN BREADS, BROWNIES AND SQUARES

Decant Layered Dessert Squares

(preheat oven to 375 degrees and lightly grease bottom of 8x8 square baking dish)

Ingredients:

(bottom layer)

¾-1 cup graham cracker crumbs

1 cup quick rolled oats

1/3 cup soften or melted vegan margarine (may add more as needed)

2-3 tablespoons non-dairy milk (any variety will work)

2-3 tablespoons pure maple syrup (may substitute with agave nectar)

(middle layer)

¾ cup crushed up shredded wheat cereal (use measurement with crushed cereal, not whole)

¾ cup no sugar added raspberry jam (strawberry jam works well too)

¾ cup creamy peanut butter (may also use almond or cashew butter)

(top layer)

1-1/2 cups melted vegan chocolate chips (may also use carob chips)

Shredded coconut (optional)

In a mixing bowl, using a fork, blend together the graham cracker crumbs, rolled oats and margarine. Slowly add in the non-dairy milk and maple syrup, starting with the smaller amounts and add more as needed, until mixture becomes well combined and slightly tacky. Press the crust mixture into the bottom only of your prepared baking dish, and bake for 12-15 minutes.

In another mixing bowl, stir together the crushed shredded wheat, jam and peanut butter until well combined. Spread evenly across baked crust, and return to oven to bake for an additional 5 minutes.

In a double boiler, slowly melt the chocolate chips, and after you've removed the cooked squares from the oven, evenly drizzle the top of the bars with the melted chocolate. Immediately sprinkle the shredded coconut onto the melted chocolate (optional), cover pan with aluminum foil and chill in the fridge for a minimum of 3 hours before cutting into squares and serving.

Autumn Spiced Pumpkin and Raisin Muffins

(preheat oven to 375 degrees and lightly grease or line 10-12 count muffin tin)

Ingredients:

2 cups flour (whole wheat)

½ cup raw sugar

1 tablespoon aluminum-free baking powder

½ teaspoon baking soda

½ teaspoon sea salt

½ teaspoon ground cinnamon

¼ teaspoon ground nutmeg

1 can (15 ounce) pumpkin puree

½ cup water

½ cup raisins

In a large mixing bowl, whisk together all the dry

ingredients until well blended. Add in the pumpkin puree, water and raisins, and stir until all ingredients are moistened and batter is well formed. Spoon batter into prepared muffin tin (each ¾ full), and bake for 25-30 minutes. Tops should spring back when lightly pressed. Remove from oven and let muffins stand for 5-7 minutes, before removing from tin and transferring to wire rack or plate to fully cool.

Nutty Chocolate Chip Brownies

(preheat oven to 350 degrees and lightly grease and flour a 9x13 inch baking dish)

Ingredients:

1 cup canola oil

1 cup pure maple syrup (do NOT use pancake syrup)

½ cup non-dairy milk (I prefer nut or oat milk for this recipe, but any variety will work)

1 tablespoon pure vanilla extract

1 cup whole wheat pastry flour

1 cup all-purpose flour

1 cup unsweetened cocoa powder

1-1/4 cups raw sugar

2 tablespoons aluminum-free baking powder

1-1/2 teaspoons sea salt

1 cup finely chopped nuts (walnuts or pecans)

1 cup vegan chocolate chips

In a mixing bowl, whisk together the canola oil, maple syrup, non-dairy milk and vanilla extract. In a separate mixing bowl, sift together both the flours, cocoa powder, sugar, baking powder and salt. Slowly fold in the dry ingredients into the wet ingredients, and stir just until all ingredients are moistened and combined. Next, fold in the chopped nuts and chocolate chips, and then transfer batter into prepared baking dish. Bake for approximately 30 minutes, or until surface cracks start to appear. Remove from oven, and place baking dish on a wire rack to cool. Brownies will finish setting as they cool, and you want to wait until brownies are fully cooled before cutting into squares.

Chocolate Chip and Walnut Biscotti

(preheat oven to 350 degrees and lightly grease a large cookie sheet)

Ingredients:

(bread)

6 tablespoons water

6 tablespoons cornstarch

1 cup canola oil

1 cup raw sugar

3-1/2 cups flour (all-purpose)

2 teaspoons aluminum-free baking powder

1 tablespoon pure vanilla extract

½-3/4 cup vegan chocolate chips

1 cup finely chopped walnuts

(sprinkled topping)

1 tablespoon raw sugar

1 tablespoon ground cinnamon

1 teaspoon cocoa powder

In a large mixing bowl, whisk together the 6 tablespoons of water and 6 tablespoons of cornstarch, to make a slurry. Add in the canola oil and sugar, and stir until sugar is dissolved. Slowly add in the flour and baking powder, a little at a time, and continue stirring until all ingredients are moistened and well combined. Fold in the vanilla extract, chocolate chips and walnuts, and stir to blend.

Once batter is mixed, divide the dough into 3 equal parts and kneed and shape each dough ball into a rectangle loaf shape, approximately 1 inch thick. (They should look like thin rectangles.) Place the rectangle dough loaves onto your prepared cookie sheet, and bake for 25 minutes. While dough is baking, whisk together the sprinkle toppings in a small bowl (raw sugar, ground cinnamon, cocoa powder). After the dough has baked for 25 minutes, remove from oven and evenly sprinkle the tops with a light dusting of the sprinkle topping. Return to oven, and bake for an additional 5 minutes. Remove from oven, cut the dough into biscotti shaped/sized pieces and turn over on the cookie sheet. Sprinkle the other side evenly with a light dusting of the sprinkle topping, and bake for a final 5 minutes. (If you like your biscotti extra firm and crunchy, flip the biscotti once more, and bake for a additional 5 minutes.) Transfer biscotti to a wire rack for cooling, then store in an airtight container.

Homestyle Apple and Oat Muffins

(preheat oven to 325 degrees and lightly grease or line a 10-12 count muffin pan)

Ingredients:

1-1/2 cups flour (all-purpose)

1-1/2 cups flour (whole wheat pastry flour)

1-1/4 teaspoons ground cinnamon

½ teaspoon ground nutmeg

½ teaspoon sea salt

2-1/2 teaspoons baking soda

1-1/2 cups quick cooking rolled oats

2 large red or green apples (peeled and finely diced)

1 container (12 ounce) thawed unsweetened apple juice concentrate (found in the freezer section)

½-3/4 cup raisins

In a large mixing bowl, sift together both the flours, cinnamon, nutmeg, salt and baking soda. Once combined, fold in the remaining ingredients, and stir just until all ingredients are moistened and well blended. Divide batter evenly, filling each muffin cup approximately ¾ full, and bake for 23-28 minutes, or until muffin tops spring back when lightly pressed. If serving muffins warm, allow to cool for 10 minutes before serving, otherwise, allow muffins to cool to room temperature and store in a tightly sealed container until ready to serve.

Super Easy Fudge Squares

(line a 8x8 inch baking dish with parchment paper, then lightly grease paper)

Ingredients:

1 cup natural peanut butter (creamy variety)

1 cup vegan chocolate chips (semi-sweet or dark)

¾ cup pure maple syrup (do NOT use pancake syrup)

1 cup finely chopped walnuts (I recommend grinding them in blender or grinder first)

Combine the peanut butter, chocolate chips and maple syrup in a saucepan over medium heat, and stir continuously until all ingredients are melted and well blended. Remove from heat and stir in the nuts. Spread batter evenly into your prepared baking dish, and chill in the fridge for a minimum of 3-4 hours before cutting into squares and serving. Not only is this the easiest fudge you'll ever make, it's addictively delicious and super quick to prepare for get-togethers, especially during the busy holiday season.

Rich and Moist Chocolate Zucchini Brownies

(preheat oven to 350 degrees and grease bottom of 8x8 inch baking dish)

Ingredients:

3 tablespoons water

1 tablespoon ground flaxseed

2 tablespoons coconut oil

2 tablespoons natural applesauce (no sugar added)

1/3 cup + 2 tablespoons of non-dairy milk (any variety will work)

½ cup raw sugar

1 teaspoon pure vanilla extract

1 cup flour (all-purpose)

1/3 cup cocoa powder (unsweetened)

¾ teaspoon baking soda

¼ teaspoon sea salt

1 overflowing cup of peeled, finely shredded zucchini (I recommend pulsing quickly in a blender or food processor – you don't want a puree, but you do want it to be finely shredded for mixing)

¾ cup vegan chocolate chips (semi-sweet or dark)

(frosting)

3-4 unsweetened cocoa powder

3-6 tablespoons non-dairy milk

½ cup pitted, chopped dates (rehydrate in water first, and then drain)

2 tablespoons coconut oil

¼ teaspoon pure vanilla extract

In a large mixing bowl, whisk together the 3 tablespoons water and 1 tablespoon ground flaxseed, and let stand for 5 minutes or so, until mixtures thickens. Once flaxseed has thickened, add in the coconut oil, applesauce, non-dairy milk, sugar and vanilla extract, and stir until all ingredients are well combined. In a separate bowl, sift together the flour, cocoa powder, baking soda and salt, and then gently fold into the bowl with the wet ingredients. Add in the zucchini and chocolate chips, and once blended, spread batter evenly into your prepared baking dish. Bake for 25-30 minutes, remove from oven and allow brownies to cool on a wire rack. The baked brownies will appear quite moist when first taken out of the oven, but will firm during cooling.

While brownies are cooling, prepare the frosting by combining all the frosting ingredients together in a blender or food processor, and puree until smooth. If frosting is too stiff, add in extra non-dairy milk, a little at a time, until desired consistency is reached. Chill frosting in the fridge while brownies are cooling. Once brownies are completely cooled, frost, cut and serve.

CHAPTER 5 – VEGAN NO-COOK, RAW DESSERTS

Raw Protein Balls

Ingredients:

½ cup raw almonds

½ cup raw pumpkin seeds

1 cup raw sunflower seeds

2 cups raisins (dark or golden)

4 tablespoons raw cocoa powder

8 tablespoons shredded coconut

1 teaspoon pure vanilla extract

Soak all the nuts and seeds in a bowl of water overnight. The next day, drain the bowl of soaked nuts and seeds, and spread them out on some paper towels to soak up any excess moisture. Next, place the nuts and seeds in a blender or food processor, and pulse/blend until mixture starts to form a coarse paste. (You may need to scrape the sides occasionally with a spatula or spoon.) Add in the remaining ingredients, and blend until mixture resembles a tacky paste. (You may again need to occasionally scrape the side with a spoon.) Form the mixture into balls (big or small) and store them in a tightly sealed container, either at room temperature or in the fridge. These make excellent energy/protein snacks to take along with you when hiking, biking, exercising, or even road trips. (I do not add sugar or stevia into this recipe, but if you like a little extra sweetness, feel free to add some in to taste.)

My Granddaughter's Favorite Chocolate Banana Cream Pie

(you'll need a 8 inch pie pan)

Ingredients:

(pie crust)

5 cups dates (pitted, and finely chopped)

1-1/2 cups raw almonds

¼ cup agave nectar

(pie filling)

4 large, semi-ripe bananas (you don't want them green, and you don't want them too soft)

1 teaspoon ground cinnamon

2 tablespoon agave nectar

¼ cup raw cocoa powder

Juice from ½ of a large lemon

1 extra banana for garnish (peeled and cut into even rounds)

To prepare the crust, combine the dates, almonds and ¼ cup agave nectar in a blender or food processor, and blend/puree until mixture starts to clump and form a paste-like consistency. Spoon out the crust mixture, and using your hands and the back of a spoon, press and form the paste along the bottom and sides of the pie pan to form the crust.

To prepare the pie filling, peel and diced the bananas, and combine them in a blender along with the remaining ingredients. Blend until smooth, and then pour the filling into your prepared pie crust. Cover with foil and place pie in freezer to set (a minimum of 3-4 hours). When ready to serve, remove pie from freezer and let stand at room temperature for about 10 minutes. Top with the banana rounds for garnish, slice and serve.

German Apple Cake Bites

(line a cookie or baking sheet with parchment paper)

Ingredients:

4 cups dried apple rings (the soft kind, not hard or crisp – I get mine in the bulk food section)

2 cups raw walnuts (measure walnuts after they are chopped, not before)

1 cup raisins (golden or dark)

10 large dates (pitted and chopped)

2 teaspoons ground cinnamon

Place the walnuts in a blender or food processor, and pulse until finely chopped. (Be careful not to over-pulse, because otherwise it will turn into walnut flour. You need to retain the nut texture.) After nuts have been finely chopped, add in the remaining ingredients, and blend/puree until mixture is well blended and starts to form a paste-like consistency. (If your mixture isn't coming together in a paste-like consistency, you may need to add in an extra date or two.) Once blended, shape the dough into 1 inch balls and arrange in a single layer on your parchment-lined baking sheet. Chill the apple cake bites in the fridge for 1-2 hours before serving. Keep apple cake bites stored in an airtight container in the fridge. These make the perfect accompaniment to a cup of fresh-brewed coffee or tea.

Apricot 'Kreme' Puffs

Ingredients:

10 fresh apricots (cut into halves and pitted)

1 cup dried apricots (soaked in water for 2 hours, drained and finely chopped)

1 cup raw macadamia nuts

½ cup water

1 to 1-1/2 tablespoons pure maple syrup

Pinch of ground cinnamon

Combine the macadamia nuts, water and maple syrup in a food processor, and puree until smooth. Transfer mixture into a mixing bowl, and stir in the chopped apricots and ground cinnamon. Arrange the fresh apricot halves on a cookie or baking sheet, and fill each one with a dollop of the apricot 'kreme'. Keep stored in the fridge until ready to serve.

Raw Maple Walnut Fudge

(line a cookie sheet with parchment paper)

Ingredients:

4 cup raw walnuts

½ cup pitted, chopped dates (soaked in water for 1 hour, drained and chopped – measure when chopped)

4 tablespoons pure maple syrup (do NOT use pancake syrup)

2 teaspoons ground cinnamon

Toss the walnuts in a blender or food processor, and pulse until finely chopped. (careful not to over-pulse) Add in the remaining ingredients, and puree until mixture forms a creamy, sticky consistency. Form dough into 1 inch round balls, and arrange in a single layer on your parchment-lined cookie sheet. Chill in fridge for a minimum of 3 hours before serving. (Note: You can also just pour the mixture into a parchment lined baking dish, chill to harden, then cut into small squares when ready to serve.

CHAPTER 6 – VEGAN FROZEN TREATS

Sweet Berry Ice Pops

(need an 8 count popsicle mold and 8 popsicle sticks)

Ingredients:

3 cups fresh chopped berries (your choice to mix and match – measure after chopped)

1/3 cup unsweetened apple juice

3 tablespoons agave nectar

Combine all 3 ingredients in a blender, and puree until smooth. Pour evenly into your popsicle mold, insert popsicle sticks and freeze until solid. Depending on what type of popsicle mold you have, you may need to wait until the berry mixture is somewhat solidified before inserting the popsicle stick into the middle.

Gina 'The Veggie Goddess' Matthews

Frozen Chocolate Peanut Butter Balls

(line a large cookie or baking dish with parchment paper
– one that will fit in your freezer)

Ingredients:

½ cup non-dairy milk (sweetened variety)

4 tablespoons unsweetened cocoa powder

4 tablespoons raw sugar (may substitute with pure maple
syrup)

½ cup natural, unsweetened peanut butter (either creamy
or crunchy is fine)

1-1/2 cups rolled oats

4 teaspoons olive oil (may substitute with coconut oil)

In a saucepan over medium-low heat, whisk together the
non-dairy milk, cocoa powder and raw sugar until sugar
is fully dissolved and ingredients are well blended.
(VERY important to whisk continuously, and not let the
mixture boil, otherwise it will curdle, and you'll need to
discard it and start over.) Turn off the heat, but keep
saucepan on burner, and stir in the peanut butter until
melted and well blended. Remove from heat and stir in
the rolled oats and olive oil. Form the batter into tightly
formed balls, and arrange them in a single layer on your
parchment-lined dish. Freeze for a minimum of 4-5
hours (covered or uncovered) before serving.

Strawberry Vanilla Ice Cream

(lightly grease bottom of 8x8 baking dish)

Ingredients:

1-1/2 cups unsweetened, non-dairy milk (coconut, rice or soy work best for this recipe)

½ cup canola oil (may substitute with grapeseed or sunflower oil)

8 tablespoons raw sugar

½ teaspoon vanilla extract

1-1/2 cups diced strawberries (fresh or frozen)

Optional Add-Ins: ½ cup finely crushed nuts / 1 tablespoon Kaluha liquor

Combine the non-dairy milk and oil in a blender, and blend at high speed for 1 minute. Add in the sugar, vanilla extract and strawberries and blend for an additional 30-60 seconds. Hand-stir in any additional add-ins at this point (nuts, liquor) if you are using them, and then transfer the mixture into your prepared baking dish. Cover with foil and place in freezer to set. To help optimize the final ice-cream consistency, give the setting ice-cream a stir after 1 hour and 2 hours in the freezer, and then let finish setting for at least another 4 hours, or overnight before serving.

Blueberry Tofu Freeze

(lightly grease bottom of 8x8 inch baking dish)

<u>Ingredients:</u>

5 cups frozen blueberries (thawed and excess water drained)

4 tablespoons pure maple syrup (may substitute with raw honey)

2 packages (12.3 ounces each) silken tofu (soft or firm)

Combine all ingredients in a blender or food processor, and puree until smooth. You may need to work the mixture in two separate batches, depending on what size blender or food processor you have. Once pureed, transfer mixture into your prepared baking dish, cover with foil and place in freezer to set, approximately 2 hours before serving.

Simple Raspberry Sorbet

(very lightly oil bottom of baking dish)

Ingredients:

2 cups water

2 cups raw sugar

1 bag (12 ounces) frozen raspberries

¼ cup fresh-squeezed lemon juice

Combine the water and sugar in a saucepan over medium heat, and stir continuously while cooking, until sugar is fully dissolved. Remove from heat, and allow mixture to cool a bit. Once sugar mixture has cooled somewhat, transfer into a blender and add in the frozen raspberries and lemon juice, and puree until smooth. Pour mixture into your prepared baking dish, cover with foil and place in the freezer to set (typically 3-4 hours). This serves nicely with an optional garnish of fresh mint leaves and/or a couple extra thawed raspberries on the side. And, in case you'd like to try this little Italian dessert trick: drizzle a very light touch (just a dab) of balsamic vinegar over your sorbet, just before eating.

CHAPTER 7 – MISCELLANEOUS VEGAN TREATS

3 Ingredient Chocolate Cream Truffles

Ingredients:

1 bag (9 ounces) vegan chocolate cream sandwich cookies (well crushed)

½ of an 8 ounce tub (you'll be using 4 ounces) vegan plain cream cheese (add more as needed)

1 bag (6 ounce) vegan bittersweet chocolate chips (melted)

Mini foil cupcake cups (liners)

In a large mixing bowl, combine the crushed cookies and cream cheese, blending until mixture becomes a pasty dough that you can shape. Add in more cream cheese if needed. Pour the already melted chocolate into a separate mixing bowl. Shape the cookie dough into teaspoon sized balls and dip in the melted chocolate to coat. Place each prepared truffle into a mini foil cupcake liner, and arrange them in a single layer on a cookie or baking sheet. For quick serve, place the truffles in the freezer for 1 hour before serving, otherwise, chill in the fridge for a minimum of 3-4 hours before serving. (These are easy to make treats to bring along to potlucks, backyard get-togethers, etc., and are definite crowd pleasers.)

Strawberry Rhubarb Cobbler

(preheat oven to 375 degrees and grease the bottom only of a 9x13 inch baking dish)

Ingredients:

2-1/2 cups diced fresh strawberries

3-1/2 cups dices fresh rhubarb

2 cups raw sugar

6 tablespoons flour (all-purpose)

1 cup packed brown sugar

1 cup rolled oats (do NOT use instant)

½ cup dry vanilla protein powder (soy or rice work best)

2 cups flour (all –purpose)

½ cup vegan margarine (softened to room temperature)

½ cup natural, unsweetened applesauce

Couple tips for this recipe: If you don't have (or want to use) the protein powder, you can substitute with an equal amount of flour. And, while many recipes that call for all-purpose flour can be substituted with whole wheat flour, in this particular recipe, using whole wheat flour can result in a very overwhelming wheat taste, therefore, I recommend only using white, all-purpose flour for this recipe.

In a mixing bowl, gently toss together the diced strawberries, diced rhubarb, 2 cups raw sugar and 6 tablespoons of flour. Make sure all ingredients are well coated, and the mixture should be a bit on the gooey side. Once mixture is thoroughly mixed, press it evenly into the bottom of your prepared baking dish. In another mixing bowl, stir together the brown sugar, rolled oats, protein powder, and 2 cups flour. After mixing, spread the dry mixture evenly across the strawberry-rhubarb layer in baking dish. Lastly, using a fork, cut together the softened margarine and applesauce, and crumble the mixture evenly across the top of the other two layers in the baking dish. Bake for 40-45 minutes, and allow cobbler to cool and set for 10 minutes before serving (if serving warm), or cover with foil or plastic wrap and store in fridge until ready to serve. Serves well with a scoop of non-dairy ice-cream.

Vegan Caramel 'Kettle' Corn

(preheat oven to 250 degrees and lightly grease a large cookie sheet)

Ingredients:

6 cups popped organic popcorn (I pop mine in an air-popper)

1 cup finely chopped pecans or almonds (you may omit if you're allergic to nuts)

2/3 cup packed brown sugar

2-3 tablespoons agave nectar

6 tablespoons vegan margarine (use the stick NOT the tub kind for this recipe)

2 tablespoons non-dairy creamer (soy or coconut-this is creamer NOT milk)

½ teaspoon sea salt

1 teaspoon pure vanilla extract

¼ teaspoon baking soda (needed to puff up the 'caramel' mixture for coating)

Have your popped popcorn and chopped nuts ready in a very large bowl. In a saucepan over medium heat, stir together the brown sugar and agave syrup, until mixture comes to a boil, being sure to stir continuously to prevent burning or sticking on the bottom of the pan.

Once mixture comes to a boil, reduce heat slightly, add in the vegan margarine, non-dairy creamer and salt, and continue cooking and whisking until mixture becomes smooth and creamy. Remove from heat and stir in the vanilla extract and baking soda. Immediately pour the 'caramel' mixture over the cooked popcorn and nuts, and toss well to evenly coat all ingredients. Spread the coated popcorn evenly on your prepared cookie sheet, and bake for 60 minutes, tossing lightly every 15 minutes. Remove from oven and serve warm, or store in an airtight container until ready to serve. (Do not attempt to bake the popcorn at a higher cooking temperature otherwise it will impart a burnt sugar flavor into the popcorn. Low and slow makes this popcorn treat come out perfect.)

Chocolate Grand Marnier Bonbons

(line a cookie sheet with parchment paper – one that will fit in your freezer)

Ingredients:

3 ounces of candied orange peel

1 tablespoon Grand Marnier liquor

10 ounces vegan chocolate chips (semi-sweet or dark)

7 tablespoons canola oil

8 ounces vegan chocolate chips (semi-sweet or dark)

In a blender or food processor, pulse together the candied orange peel and Grand Marnier until mixture becomes coarse (like wet sand), and then set aside. In a double boiler (or use a small pot over a large pot of boiling water), add the 10 ounces of chocolate chips and canola oil, and stir continuously until fully melted. Remove from heat, add in the orange peel mixture, and stir until well incorporated. Mixture will quickly start to thicken, so you need to work fast.

Transfer the mixture onto a clean cutting board, and as soon as it becomes cool enough to handle, roll the dough into approximately 1 inch sized balls and arrange them in a single layer on your parchment-lined cookie sheet. Place cookie sheet in your freezer for 2-3 hours, to allow bonbons to set. Just before you're ready to take out your bonbons, in the same double boiler, slowly melt the 8 ounces of chocolate chips, and then immediately remove from heat. Remove the bonbons from the freezer, and dip each one fully (or top half only) into the melted chocolate, and place back onto the parchment-lined cookie sheet. Once you have dipped all the bonbons, return to the freezer for 1 more hour, to allow the chocolate to harden. Once the bonbons are done, you may store them in an airtight container, in a cool place in your kitchen or in the fridge.

Easy Candied Pecans

(line a cookie sheet with parchment paper)

Ingredients:

½ cup packed brown sugar

2 tablespoons olive oil

2 tablespoons balsamic vinegar (do not substitute any other type of vinegar)

2 cups pecan halves

Combine the brown sugar, olive oil and balsamic vinegar in a skillet over medium heat, and whisk continuously until sugar is fully dissolved and mixture starts to bubble. Once mixture starts to bubble, add in the pecan halves, toss to coat evenly with the sugar mixture, and continue cooking while stirring frequently until pecans are toasted (approximately 5 minutes). Remove from heat and transfer onto your parchment-lined cookie sheet. Using a couple forks or spoons, separate the pecans while still warm (otherwise they'll clump together), and allow to fully cool. Your candied pecans will store for 3-4 weeks, if kept in an airtight container at room temperature. These little treats make great holiday gifts for your neighbors, co-workers, etc., and you can easily multiple the recipe to make in larger batches all at once.

Campfire Banana Boats

(heavy-duty foil for wrapping each serving -you can make these over a campfire, on your grill, or broiled in the oven)

Ingredients:

4 large, semi-ripe bananas (you want them firm)

½ cup vegan chocolate chips (semi-sweet or dark)

½ cup unsweetened shredded coconut

½ cup finely chopped nuts (walnuts or pecans)

Whiskey or bourbon for drizzle AFTER cooking (optional)

Cut off 4 squares of aluminum foil, large enough to fully wrap each banana, and set aside. In a mixing bowl, or large Ziploc bag, mix together the chocolate chips, shredded coconut and chopped nuts until well combined. Peel each banana, and carefully slice in half lengthwise. After you've halved the bananas, using a melon-scooper or small teaspoon, carefully carve out a small scoop line down the middle of the banana. The scooped out section helps hold the filling in place. Arrange a scooped banana half in the middle of each piece of foil, and evenly divide the filling mixture (chocolate, coconut, nuts) into the center of each banana. Place the other half of the banana on top, to make what looks like a stuffed banana sandwich, and wrap tightly with the foil. Place your banana foil packets over your campfire, grill or broiler in the oven, and cook until ingredients melt and caramelize. The hotter the fire/grill/oven, the quicker it will cook (approximately 5-7 minutes). Remove from heat source, and serve each banana foil packet on a plate with a fork. To make an adult version of this recipe, immediately after removing the banana packets from heat source, drizzle some whiskey or bourbon across the top of each stuffed banana boat. Do NOT add the whiskey or bourbon before cooking otherwise you might need to call the fire department.

'Karamel' Nut Fruit Dip

Ingredients:

2 packages (8 ounces each) vegan cream cheese (plain and softened to room temperature)

4 tablespoons raw sugar

1-1/2 cups packed brown sugar

2 tablespoons pure vanilla extract

2 cups finely chopped/crushed nuts (walnuts, pecans or peanuts) – (optional)

Fruit slices for dipping.

In a mixing bowl, beat together the cream cheese, both the sugars and vanilla extract until mixture is smooth and creamy. Hand stir in the crushed nuts (optional) and stir to blend. Cover bowl and store in fridge for a minimum of 6 hours or overnight, to allow flavor to develop. Serve with fresh cut fruit slices (apples, pears, etc.), rice cakes or even pretzels.

ADDITIONAL BOOKS BY AUTHOR

- ♦ Easy Vegetarian Cooking: 100 – 5 Ingredients or Less, Easy and Delicious Vegetarian Recipes

- ♦ Natural Foods: 100 – 5 Ingredients or Less, Raw Food Recipes for Every Meal Occasion

- ♦ Easy Vegetarian Cooking: 75 Delicious Vegetarian Casserole Recipes

- ♦ Easy Vegetarian Cooking: 75 Delicious Vegetarian Soup and Stew Recipes

- ♦ The Veggie Goddess Vegetarian Cookbook Collection: Volumes 1-4

- ♦ Easy Vegan Cooking: 100 Easy and Delicious Vegan Recipes

- ♦ Vegan Cooking: 50 Delectable Vegan Dessert Recipes

- ♦ Holiday Vegan Recipes: Holiday Menu Planning for Halloween through New Years

- ♦ Natural Cures: 200 All Natural Fruit & Veggie Remedies for Weight Loss, Health and Beauty

ABOUT THE AUTHOR

Gina 'The Veggie Goddess' Matthews, resides in sunny Phoenix, Arizona, and has been a lover of animals, nature, gardening and, of course, vegetarian cuisine since childhood. 'The Veggie Goddess' strongly encourages home gardening, supporting your local farmers and organic food co-ops, preserving the well-being of Mother Earth, and supporting and protecting animal rights.

Printed in Great Britain
by Amazon

39257059R00056